Quran Stories for
Little Believers

I See Allah Everywhere

by

S A N I Y A S N A I N   K H A N

Goodword**kidz**

Helping you build a family of faith

Up in the sky.

2

4

When it rains.

5

In the forest.

When the sun shines.

Over the mountains.

In the flowers.

Under the sea.

14

I see Allah everywhere.